Deborah McCann

# Let Us Gather

*Prayer Services
for Catholic Schools
and Assemblies*

**TWENTY-THIRD PUBLICATIONS**

185 WILLOW STREET • PO BOX 180 • MYSTIC, CT 06355
TEL: 1-800-321-0411 • FAX: 1-800-572-0788
E-MAIL: ttpubs@aol.com • www.twentythirdpublications.com

# Dedication

To all the people I pray with and pray for:
your witness is a continuing challenge and grace.

The Scripture passages contained herein are from the *New Revised Standard Version of the Bible,* copyright ©1989, by the Division of Christian Education of the National Council of Churches of Christ in the U.S.A. All rights reserved. Scripture quotations marked (CEV) are from the *Contemporary English Version Bible,* copyright © American Bible Society, 1995, 1999.

Twenty-Third Publications
A Division of Bayard
185 Willow Street
P.O. Box 180
Mystic, CT 06355
(860) 536-2611
(800) 321-0411
www.twentythirdpublications.com

ISBN:1-58595-213-3
Library of Congress Catalog Card Number: 2002103863
Printed in the U.S.A.

# Contents

# Introduction

One day my son's third-grade teacher approached me and asked if I knew of any prayer services that could be used as part of Say No to Drugs Week. I went home and looked through many books, finding nothing. Then the idea hit—I could write a prayer service and tailor it to the schoolchildren (intercessory prayer, one petition per grade, pre-K through 8). I wrote one and handed it in.

That was the beginning of a burgeoning "cottage industry." Since then I have provided prayer services for teacher appreciation days, May crownings, and special days of prayer. I offer this book to any busy prayer leader who might need some suggestions for prayers that reflect different seasons and cycles of the church and school year, as well as issues that touch deeply those we teach. My thanks go to all the teachers at St. Mary Star of the Sea School in New London, Connecticut, who provided the holy ground where many of these prayers grew. Special thanks to Cathy Santangelo, who got me started, and to my husband, Dan, and my son, Michael, who have been a constant inspiration and reminder of God's love and presence among us.

## Praying the Prayers

The prayers follow a simple format: a call to prayer, a reading from Scripture, intercessions, and a closing prayer. There are intercessions for each grade from pre-K through 8. Though developed around the structure of a parochial school, these services can be cut or adapted easily depending on the makeup of your school or religious education program. I have tried to make them as universal as possible, bearing in mind that not every prayer service will fit every situation. For example, I offer four prayers for seasons of the year; I realize not everyone using this book will find all of these applicable. And that's fine. I offer these services as is or as a starting point to spur your own imagination.

The format is simple enough to follow, and only those offering intercessions and doing the readings really need to have a copy of the service. When choosing readers, it is always a good idea to choose children who want to read. I found it very helpful to ask older siblings of those in pre-K and Kindergarten to read the petitions with their brothers and sisters. It's important that these prayers never be a source of tension or an uncomfortable duty, but a chance to really think about and celebrate all the ways we can praise God.

I have started each prayer with a simple Sign of the Cross greeting. This is, of course, a perfectly fine way to begin. As the year progresses, though, and the children start to become more familiar and comfortable with this prayer format, you might want to consider using alternate beginnings (which will also subtly introduce other parts of Scripture to them).

For example:

| | |
|---|---|
| Leader | This is the day the Lord has made. |
| All | Let us rejoice and be glad. |
| | |
| Leader | Our help is in the name of the Lord. |
| All | Who made heaven and earth. |
| | |
| Leader | God, come to my assistance. |
| All | Lord, make haste to help me. |
| | |
| Leader | Blessed be God. |
| All | Blessed be God's holy name. |
| | |
| Leader | Let us praise the Lord. |
| All | Now and forever. |
| | |
| Leader | Bless the Lord, O my soul. |
| All | And all my being praise God's holy name. |
| | |
| Leader | The Lord has done great things for us. |
| All | We are filled with joy. |
| | |
| Leader | Give thanks to the Lord, for he is good. |
| All | His mercy endures forever. |
| | |
| Leader | Lord, open our lips. |
| All | And our mouths will proclaim your praise. |
| | |
| Leader | Lord, send out your Spirit. |
| All | And renew the face of the earth. |

I hope you will find these prayer services useful and fun to do. However you use them, in whole or in part, the important message is that God's word is alive and waiting to speak to us. Let us gather and begin to listen!

# Seasons of School Life

Here, from the first day of school to the last, is a collection of prayer services that can be used throughout the school year. They emphasize community and cooperation, whether it involves doing schoolwork, sending classmates off to represent the school, or gathering to support those with sickness in their families. There is also a service to be said as a blessing for the parish  (a prayerful way to bring church and school communities together).

 # Let Us Gather

**New school year**

Teachers may want to do the petitions for this prayer. It would be a good way for their youngsters to get to know them.

**Call to Prayer**

Leader     In the name of the Father, and of the Son, and of the Holy Spirit.

All     Amen.

Leader     Let us gather eagerly and with joy to begin the new school year, a year filled with all kinds of new things to learn and new ways to grow. In all our work and effort this year, let us keep one goal in mind: to show always and everywhere our joy at being children of God.

**Reading**     **Philippians 4:4–9**

Reader 1     Rejoice in the Lord always; again I will say, Rejoice. Let your gentleness be known to everyone. The Lord is near.

Reader 2     Do not worry about anything, but in everything by prayer and supplication with thanksgiving let your requests be made known to God. And the peace of God, which surpasses all understanding, will guard your hearts and your minds in Christ Jesus.

Reader 3     Finally, whatever is true, whatever is honorable, whatever is just, whatever is pure, whatever is pleasing, whatever is commendable, if there is any excellence and if there is anything worthy of praise, think about these things.

Reader 4     Keep on doing the things that you have learned and received and heard and seen, and the God of peace will be with you.

Leader     We come before you, Lord, to offer ourselves to you in everything we do. Hear us as we pray: Lead us on your way.

All     Lead us on your way.

## Intercessions

| | |
|---|---|
| Pre-K | We offer you ourselves in our work and in our play. |
| All | Lead us on your way. |
| K | We offer you ourselves in our care for one another. |
| All | Lead us on your way. |
| Grade 1 | We offer you ourselves in our desire to learn. |
| All | Lead us on your way. |
| Grade 2 | We offer you ourselves in our joy at learning new things. |
| All | Lead us on your way. |
| Grade 3 | We offer you ourselves in our struggles with new subjects. |
| All | Lead us on your way. |
| Grade 4 | We offer you ourselves in our wonder at your world. |
| All | Lead us on your way. |
| Grade 5 | We offer you ourselves in our search for answers to hard questions. |
| All | Lead us on your way. |
| Grade 6 | We offer you ourselves in our prayers and celebrations. |
| All | Lead us on your way. |
| Grade 7 | We offer you ourselves in our time of rapid growing. |
| All | Lead us on your way. |
| Grade 8 | We offer you ourselves in our hearts and in our lives. |
| All | Lead us on your way. |
| | |
| Leader | Dear God, your love and care strengthen us always. Help us respond to your love by seeing your face in everyone we meet. Make this year wholesome and productive, where questions are raised and answered, knowledge grows, and prayers are heartfelt and free. We ask this in the confidence given us by your Son, our Savior, Jesus Christ, whose example is our shining model. |
| All | Amen. |

# Remember, I Am With You

**For those who represent the school in other places**

This prayer service can be used to offer good wishes and support to sports teams, those going to history, science, or arts fairs; regional band meets or choruses—or other groups taking the school or parish's spirit into the world.

**Call to Prayer**

| | |
|---|---|
| Leader | In the name of the Father, and of the Son, and of the Holy Spirit. |
| All | Amen. |
| Leader | We gather today to send forth our (name team, or representatives, i.e., baseball team, science finalists) in the name of our school (parish). We wish them blessings on their way, and the wisdom to accept as a moment of grace whatever the outcome may be. We bless them with Jesus' command to his disciples: |

**Reading**     **Matthew 28:16–20**

| | |
|---|---|
| Reader 1 | Now the eleven disciples went to Galilee, to the mountain to which Jesus had directed them. |
| Reader 2 | When they saw him, they worshipped him; but some doubted. |
| Reader 3 | And Jesus came and said to them, |
| Reader 4 | "All authority in heaven and on earth has been given to me. Go therefore and make disciples of all nations, baptizing them in the name of the Father and of the Son and of the Holy Spirit, and teaching them to obey everything that I have commanded you. |
| Readers 1-4 | And remember, I am with you always, to the end of the age." |
| Leader | We send you forth in the grace of God, wishing you confidence, success, and most of all, joy in this chance to share your gifts with others. May you and those you meet all be enriched by this sharing. Let us respond: May God be with you. |
| All | May God be with you. |

## Intercessions

| | |
|---|---|
| Pre-K | We hope you have a wonderful time. |
| All | May God be with you. |
| K | We hope you return with lots of stories to tell. |
| All | May God be with you. |
| Grade 1 | We hope your trip, both going and coming, is safe and fun. |
| All | May God be with you. |
| Grade 2 | We hope you remember everything you are supposed to do and say. |
| All | May God be with you. |
| Grade 3 | We hope you enjoy meeting other people with the same talents you have. |
| All | May God be with you. |
| Grade 4 | We hope this will be a time of great sharing, fun, and learning. |
| All | May God be with you. |
| Grade 5 | We hope you have success, maybe by winning, but certainly by growing. |
| All | May God be with you. |
| Grade 6 | We hope you have eyes to see and ears to hear what God will tell you on your journey. |
| All | May God be with you. |
| Grade 7 | We hope you rejoice in the fellowship that comes from good sportsmanship. |
| All | May God be with you. |
| Grade 8 | We hope your skills and talents and gifts are celebrated by others as we celebrate you. |
| All | May God be with you. |
| | |
| Leader | Dear Lord, we place our young people in your hands, knowing that you will take good care of them. Keep them safe and walk with them, as they go forth to serve you with gladness. Help them feel our support and our pride in them, and let them glory in all the adventures this trip will bring. Whatever the outcome, help them know your grace and love. |
| All | Amen. |

# Take and Bear Our Fears

**For those with sickness in their families**

Children—and adults—with sickness in their families are often frightened and feel very much alone. This service is offered as a sign of solidarity with their suffering and uncertainty.

**Call to Prayer**

| | |
|---|---|
| Leader | In the name of the Father, and of the Son, and of the Holy Spirit. |
| All | Amen. |
| Leader | We gather today to offer our love and support to (name person or persons) because his (her) (name relative or friend) is sick. We want to pray for them and for their whole family, because this can be such a frightening and uncertain time. Let us remember this story from the gospel: |

**Reading**    **Matthew 8:14–17**

| | |
|---|---|
| Reader 1 | When Jesus entered Peter's house, he saw his mother-in-law lying in bed with a fever. |
| Reader 2 | He touched her hand, and the fever left her, and she got up and began to serve him. |
| Reader 3 | That evening they brought to him many who were possessed by demons; and he cast out the spirits with a word, and cured all who were sick. |
| Reader 4 | This was to fulfill what had been spoken through the prophet Isaiah, "He took our infirmities and bore our diseases." |
| | |
| Leader | Good and gracious God, please watch over (name)'s (relative). She (he) is frightened but not alone, because all of us here stand with her (him) in her (his) time of need. |
| | [Leader may invite all those present to extend their right hand in blessing toward the person(s) being prayed for.] |
| | Bless (name) and his (her) whole family. Help them remember the joy of health and well-being. Hear us as we pray: Lord, take and bear our fears. |
| All | Lord, take and bear our fears. |

**Intercessions**

| | |
|---|---|
| Pre-K | May sadness go away. |
| All | Lord, take and bear our fears. |
| K | May love hold you close. |
| All | Lord, take and bear our fears. |
| Grade 1 | May healing come like sunrise every day. |
| All | Lord, take and bear our fears. |
| Grade 2 | May hope comfort you. |
| All | Lord, take and bear our fears. |
| Grade 3 | May grace surround you. |
| All | Lord, take and bear our fears. |
| Grade 4 | May rest refresh you. |
| All | Lord, take and bear our fears. |
| Grade 5 | May fear be banished. |
| All | Lord, take and bear our fears. |
| Grade 6 | May God the Father bless you and all those you love. |
| All | Lord, take and bear our fears. |
| Grade 7 | May God the Son walk with you in sorrow and in joy. |
| All | Lord, take and bear our fears. |
| Grade 8 | May God the Holy Spirit fill your soul with peace. |
| All | Lord, take and bear our fears. |

| | |
|---|---|
| Leader | Good and gracious God, we place ourselves in your hands. All of us hope for healing and hope and joy for (name) and her (his) family. Give us the grace to welcome you in our lives, to offer help and comfort in your name, and to praise the miracles you perform for us each and every day. |
| All | Amen. |

 # Benediction

**For the parish**

This prayer service may be offered at times of parish renewal, or in support of National Clergy Month (October), Administrative Professionals Week (April), or at any other occasion when the parish staff and parish community should be recognized and affirmed.

**Call to Prayer**

| | |
|---|---|
| Leader | In the name of the Father, and of the Son, and of the Holy Spirit. |
| All | Amen. |
| Leader | We gather together to offer our prayer and our blessing on all those in our parish community, those who work here, those who worship here, and those who guide us in our journey of faith. Let our spirits echo the wise counsel of the apostle Paul. |

**Reading**  1 Thessalonians 5:18, 22 (CEV)

| | |
|---|---|
| Reader 1 | My friends, we ask you to be thoughtful of your leaders who work hard and tell you how to live for the Lord. |
| Reader 2 | Show them great respect and love because of their work. Try to get along with each other. |
| Reader 3 | My friends, we beg you to warn anyone who is not living right. |
| Reader 4 | Encourage anyone who feels left out, help all who are weak, and be patient with everyone. Be good to each other and to everyone else. |
| Readers 1-4 | Always be joyful and never stop praying. Whatever happens, keep thanking God because of Jesus Christ. |
| Readers 1-2 | This is what God wants you to do. |
| Readers 3-4 | Accept what is good and don't have anything to do with evil. |
| Leader | God, our Good Shepherd, guide us all in love. Help our priests and our workers, our religious and our teachers, our elderly and our children, our faithful and those who have doubts and fears. We are all your family, and we come here in this place to offer our prayers. Hear us as we say: Bless them, O Lord. |
| All | Bless them, O Lord. |

**Intercessions**

| | |
|---|---|
| Pre-K | For those who teach us |
| All | Bless them, O Lord. |
| K | For those who watch us on the playground |
| All | Bless them, O Lord. |
| Grade 1 | For those who work in the lunchroom |
| All | Bless them, O Lord. |
| Grade 2 | For those who help us learn about God |
| All | Bless them, O Lord. |
| Grade 3 | For those who mow the lawns and plant the flowers |
| All | Bless them, O Lord. |
| Grade 4 | For those who answer phones and type letters |
| All | Bless them, O Lord. |
| Grade 5 | For those whose words guide and inspire us |
| All | Bless them, O Lord. |
| Grade 6 | For those who praise your name each day |
| All | Bless them, O Lord. |
| Grade 7 | For those who need our help and strength |
| All | Bless them, O Lord. |
| Grade 8 | For those who give us a model to live by, and a safe haven from our fears |
| All | Bless them, O Lord. |

| | |
|---|---|
| Leader | O Lord, we thank you for all these people who make our parish what it is. Keep us all holy and blameless in your sight. Help us rejoice, support one another, and give thanks. Open our ears to listen as well as to hear. Help us see you in everyone we meet. Send us forth into the world confidently and with open hearts because of all that you have done for us. We ask this through your Son, Jesus, our Lord. |
| All | Amen. |

# Let Us Go In Peace

**End of school year**

By this time children should be used to the prayer format and structure, and should be able to do the petitions themselves. For the younger grades, of course, you still might want to choose a child from an older grade to read on their behalf—an older sibling, perhaps.

**Call to Prayer**

| | |
|---|---|
| Leader | In the name of the Father, and of the Son, and of the Holy Spirit. |
| All | Amen. |
| Leader | Our school year is ended. The year that stretched out so long before us last September has faded to this day, a day blessed with the taste of summer and the promise of lazy days and good times ahead. As we prepare to scatter for vacation, let us remember what we have learned, and what we can carry forth to the world around us—the word and work of our Lord. |

| | |
|---|---|
| **Reading** | **1 Corinthians 2:5–10, 12 (CEV)** |
| Reader 1 | You have faith because of God's power and not because of human wisdom. We do use wisdom when speaking to people who are mature in their faith. But it is not the wisdom of this world or of its rulers. |
| Reader 2 | We speak of God's hidden and mysterious wisdom that God decided to use for our glory long before the world began. The rulers of this world didn't know anything about this wisdom. If they had known about it, they would not have nailed the glorious Lord to a cross. |
| Reader 3 | But it is just as the Scriptures say: "What God has planned for people who love him is more than eyes have seen or ears have heard. It has never even entered our minds." |
| Reader 4 | God's Spirit has shown you everything. And God has given us his Spirit. That's why we don't think the same way that people of this world think. That's also why we can recognize the blessings that God has given us. |
| Leader | As summer beckons, full of fun and good times, let us thank the Lord for all the goodness shown us this year, as we respond, Thank you, Lord. |
| All | Thank you, Lord. |

**Intercessions**

| | |
|---|---|
| Pre-K | For the things we learned all year |
| All | Thank you, Lord. |
| K | For the people we have met |
| All | Thank you, Lord. |
| Grade 1 | For our teachers and their patience |
| All | Thank you, Lord. |
| Grade 2 | For the wonders of your world |
| All | Thank you, Lord. |
| Grade 3 | For the sciences and arts |
| All | Thank you, Lord. |
| Grade 4 | For the history of all people |
| All | Thank you, Lord. |
| Grade 5 | For the promise of good times |
| All | Thank you, Lord. |
| Grade 6 | For the snow days and the spring days |
| All | Thank you, Lord. |
| Grade 7 | For the friends we've made and cherished |
| All | Thank you, Lord. |
| Grade 8 | For your love that we have known here |
| All | Thank you, Lord. |

| | |
|---|---|
| Leader | Dear Lord, your blessings are too many to count. Thank you for all those we have just named, and those within our hearts. Keep our young people safe as they play and grow this summer. Guide those who are leaving us; may we stay close to them in thought and prayer. Keep us all healthy and happy so we can greet you with joy when vacation is over and school begins again. For all your blessings, for your saving power, for your amazing love, we thank you, Lord. |
| All | Amen. |

# Seasons of the Year

Any time is appropriate for praising God, but perhaps one of the most natural occasions is at the change of seasons. With some adaptation, any of these would be useful at some time in your year.

 # We Celebrate You

**Autumn**

Autumn offers so many opportunities to praise God. This service would be fine to use anytime between the beginning of school and Thanksgiving.

**Call to Prayer**

| | |
|---|---|
| Leader | In the name of the Father, and of the Son, and of the Holy Spirit. |
| All | Amen. |
| Leader | The days are growing shorter, the trees are dressed in their loveliest colors, and the air has grown crisp and brisk. We gather to thank God for these changes, for the glory of the seasons, and for the wonder that each season brings to our lives. |

**Reading**   Psalm 8:1, 3–6

| | |
|---|---|
| Readers 1-4 | O Lord, our Sovereign, how majestic is your name in all the earth! |
| Reader 1 | You have set your glory above the heavens. |
| Reader 2 | When I look at your heavens, the work of your fingers, |
| Reader 3 | the moon and the stars that you have established; |
| Reader 4 | what are human beings that you are mindful of them? |
| Readers 1-4 | O Lord, our Sovereign, how majestic is your name in all the earth! |
| Reader 1 | Yet you have made them a little lower than God, |
| Reader 2 | you have crowned them with glory and honor. |
| Reader 3 | You have given them dominion over the works of your hands; |
| Reader 4 | you have put all things under their feet. |
| Readers 1-4 | O Lord, our Sovereign, how majestic is your name in all the earth! |

| | |
|---|---|
| Leader | Lord of all, we welcome these fine days. As we turn our thoughts toward harvest, the ever chillier air, and more time indoors, let us welcome the changes around us. Hear us as we pray: We celebrate you, O Lord. |
| All | We celebrate you, O Lord. |

**Intercessions**

| | |
|---|---|
| Pre-K | When we think of the pretty leaves |
| All | We celebrate you, O Lord. |
| K | When we think of the shorter days |
| All | We celebrate you, O Lord. |
| Grade 1 | When we think of the darker nights |
| All | We celebrate you, O Lord. |
| Grade 2 | When we think of the cooler weather |
| All | We celebrate you, O Lord. |
| Grade 3 | When we think of huddling under blankets |
| All | We celebrate you, O Lord. |
| Grade 4 | When we think of Halloween and trick or treat |
| All | We celebrate you, O Lord. |
| Grade 5 | When we think of your autumn saints, like Francis |
| All | We celebrate you, O Lord. |
| Grade 6 | When we think of all your saints |
| All | We celebrate you, O Lord. |
| Grade 7 | When we think of your goodness in blessing us with seasons |
| All | We celebrate you, O Lord. |
| Grade 8 | When we think of the miracle of life even as the earth settles to sleep |
| All | We celebrate you, O Lord. |
| | |
| Leader | We celebrate you, O Lord, in everything that we do. Keep us close to you and help us to see your goodness and bounty always and everywhere. |
| All | Amen. |

 # We Glorify You

**Winter**

This prayer service was designed for the long, cold months of January and February, when snow days are prayed for and the winter doldrums have set in.

**Call to Prayer**

| | |
|---|---|
| Leader | In the name of the Father, and of the Son, and of the Holy Spirit. |
| All | Amen. |
| Leader | Night is now longer than day, the trees are bare, and we shiver with the cold. We gather to thank God for these changes, for the glory of the seasons, and for the wonder that each season brings to our lives. |

**Reading**     **Sirach 43:13, 17–20, 27–29**

| | |
|---|---|
| Reader 1 | By his command, God sends the driving snow. |
| Reader 2 | He scatters the snow like birds flying down, |
| Reader 3 | and its descent is like locusts alighting. |
| Reader 4 | The eye is dazzled by the beauty of its whiteness, and the mind is amazed as it falls. |
| Reader 1 | He pours frost over the earth like salt, |
| Reader 2 | and icicles form like pointed thorns. |
| Reader 3 | The cold north wind blows, and ice freezes on the water. |
| Reader 4 | It settles on every pool of water, and the water puts it on like a breastplate. |
| Reader 1 | We could say more but could never say enough. |
| Reader 2 | Let the final word be |
| Readers 1-4 | "He is the all." |
| Reader 3 | Where can we find the strength to praise him? |
| Reader 4 | For he is greater than all his works. |
| Readers 1-4 | Awesome is the Lord and very great, and marvelous is his power. |

| | |
|---|---|
| Leader | Awesome are you, Lord, and we praise the wonder of your world. Even now in the frost and chill outside there are hints of the sun's warming touch. Hear us as we praise you, saying: We glorify you, Lord. |
| All | We glorify you, Lord. |

## Intercessions

| | |
|---|---|
| Pre-K | We glorify you for cold nights and warm hugs. |
| All | We glorify you, Lord. |
| K | We glorify you for hot chocolate and warm mittens. |
| All | We glorify you, Lord. |
| Grade 1 | We glorify you for snow days and snowballs. |
| All | We glorify you, Lord. |
| Grade 2 | We glorify you for sleds and steep hills. |
| All | We glorify you, Lord. |
| Grade 3 | We glorify you for sweaters and scarves and warm coats. |
| All | We glorify you, Lord. |
| Grade 4 | We glorify you for sun shining on snow and crisp blue skies. |
| All | We glorify you, Lord. |
| Grade 5 | We glorify you for breath we can see and rosy red cheeks. |
| All | We glorify you, Lord. |
| Grade 6 | We glorify you for the chance to help others on snowy days. |
| All | We glorify you, Lord. |
| Grade 7 | We glorify you for the beauty of icicles and snow drifts. |
| All | We glorify you, Lord. |
| Grade 8 | We glorify you for your love, which shares these blessings with us all. |
| All | We glorify you, Lord. |
| | |
| Leader | Lord, in this season of cold and darkness, help us to see the promise of the season to come, even as we enjoy the gifts of winter. Help us to appreciate the gifts you offer that make winter so special. May we never forget all those in need this winter. We glorify you, Lord, in all that we do. |
| All | Amen. |

# Making a Joyful Noise

**Spring**

Spring offers us a chance to rejoice in the rebirth of the world, the return of light and warmth, and the glory of the resurrection.

**Call to Prayer**

| | |
|---|---|
| Leader | In the name of the Father, and of the Son, and of the Holy Spirit. |
| All | Amen. |
| Leader | We gather today to celebrate God's wonderful gift of spring. Daylight is with us longer, the trees are budding with new life, and we begin to feel again the warmth of the sun. We gather to thank God for these changes, for the glory of the seasons, and for the wonder that each season brings to our lives. |

**Reading**  **Psalm 98:1, 3, 4–8**

| | |
|---|---|
| Reader 1 | O sing to the Lord a new song, for he has done marvelous things. |
| Reader 2 | All the ends of the earth have seen the victory of our God. |
| Reader 3 | Make a joyful noise to the Lord, all the earth; |
| Reader 4 | break forth into joyous song and sing praises. |
| Readers 1-4 | All the ends of the earth have seen the victory of our God. |
| Reader 1 | Sing praises to the Lord with the lyre, |
| Reader 2 | with the lyre and the sound of melody. |
| Reader 3 | With trumpets and the sound of the horn |
| Reader 4 | make a joyful noise before the King, the Lord. |
| Readers 1-4 | All the ends of the earth have seen the victory of our God. |
| Reader 1 | Let the sea roar, and all that fills it; |
| Reader 2 | the world and those who live in it. |
| Reader 3 | Let the floods clap their hands; |
| Reader 4 | let the hills sing together for joy. |
| Readers 1-4 | All the ends of the earth have seen the victory of our God. |

| | |
|---|---|
| Leader | Dear Lord, in this season when we celebrate resurrection, we praise you for these rare and wonderful days, saying: We're here to make a joyful noise. |
| All | We're here to make a joyful noise. |

**Intercessions**

| | |
|---|---|
| Pre-K | For the flower buds and new green leaves |
| All | We're here to make a joyful noise. |
| K | For the longer days and warmer sun |
| All | We're here to make a joyful noise. |
| Grade 1 | For the extra play time we have each day |
| All | We're here to make a joyful noise. |
| Grade 2 | For baseball and for time outdoors |
| All | We're here to make a joyful noise. |
| Grade 3 | For kickball and for jump rope |
| All | We're here to make a joyful noise. |
| Grade 4 | For soccer and for sidewalk chalk |
| All | We're here to make a joyful noise. |
| Grade 5 | For piles of coats and the air in our faces |
| All | We're here to make a joyful noise. |
| Grade 6 | For the birds and the bugs and the butterflies |
| All | We're here to make a joyful noise. |
| Grade 7 | For the glory of Easter and its fifty days of joy |
| All | We're here to make a joyful noise. |
| Grade 8 | For the promise and wonder of our world |
| All | We're here to make a joyful noise. |

Leader Dear Lord, we come before you filled once again with energy and hope. In the signs you give us, we see your love and mercy. As we glory in your goodness, help us always remember those in need, and guide us to do what we can to help them. Thank you for the glories of this season, and for the amazing and wonderful gift of your Son.

All Amen.

# Praise the Lord!

**Summer**

This prayer service is designed to be used any time before the end of school, or perhaps even during a vacation Bible school. With adaptation of the call to prayer, it could be used any time at all.

**Call to Prayer**

| Leader | In the name of the Father, and of the Son, and of the Holy Spirit. |
| --- | --- |
| All | Amen. |
| Leader | We gather to celebrate the wonders of summer. We have endless hours before us of light and warmth. The trees are full of leaves that shade us and send us breezes, and the air has grown hot but comforting. We gather to thank God for these changes, for the glory of the seasons, and for the wonder that each season brings to our lives. |

**Reading   Psalm 148**

| Readers 1-4 | Praise the Lord! |
| --- | --- |
| Reader 1 | Praise the Lord from the heavens; praise him in the heights! |
| Reader 2 | Praise him, all his angels; praise him, all his hosts! |
| Readers 1-4 | Praise the Lord! |
| Reader 3 | Praise him, sun and moon; praise him, all you shining stars! |
| Reader 4 | Praise him, you highest heavens, and you waters above the heavens! |
| Readers 1-4 | Praise the Lord! |
| Reader 1 | Let them praise the name of the Lord, for he commanded and they were created. |
| Reader 2 | He established them for ever and ever; he fixed their bounds, which cannot be passed. |
| Readers 1-4 | Praise the Lord! |
| Reader 3 | Praise the name of the Lord, |
| Reader 4 | for his name alone is exalted; |
| Readers 1-4 | Praise the Lord! |

| Leader | God of all good, we welcome these warm and happy days, full of promise and wonder. Hear us as we pray: Praise the Lord! |
| --- | --- |
| All | Praise the Lord! |

## Intercessions

| | |
|---|---|
| Pre-K | For time to play |
| All | Praise the Lord! |
| K | For time to blow bubbles |
| All | Praise the Lord! |
| Grade 1 | For vacation |
| All | Praise the Lord! |
| Grade 2 | For long summer days |
| All | Praise the Lord! |
| Grade 3 | For the flowers and the butterflies |
| All | Praise the Lord! |
| Grade 4 | For the birds and the squirrels |
| All | Praise the Lord! |
| Grade 5 | For the wonders of our planet |
| All | Praise the Lord! |
| Grade 6 | For the beauty of the earth |
| All | Praise the Lord! |
| Grade 7 | For the chance to give you praise |
| All | Praise the Lord! |
| Grade 8 | For the wonder that is You |
| All | Praise the Lord! |

| | |
|---|---|
| Leader | Dear Lord, we praise you for your goodness, for our time together, and for the summer that lies before us, just waiting to be filled with good things. Keep us safe and healthy and happy, Lord, so that we may serve you in joy. |
| All | Amen. |

# Seasons of the Church Year

**M**any of the major seasons of the church year occur during the school year. From All Saints and All Souls, from Advent through Christmas and Epiphany, from Lent through Easter and Pentecost, there are all kinds of occasions when you can help children reflect on and celebrate the wonderful gifts of God expressed in each of these seasons.

# Godly People, Communion of Saints

**All Saints, All Souls**

This service may be used for both All Saints Day and All Souls Day. It will give children a chance to think of the members of their own families who are members of the communion of saints—themselves included! Note: the Scripture has been adapted to refer to all present.

**Call to Prayer**

| | |
|---|---|
| Leader | In the name of the Father, and of the Son, and of the Holy Spirit. |
| All | Amen. |
| Leader | Dear Lord, thanks to your redeeming love, we are all members of the communion of saints—all of us here, and all who have gone before us. We give you glory as we hear the words from the Book of Sirach. |

**Reading**     **Sirach 44:1–6, 10–11, 13 (CEV)**

| | |
|---|---|
| Reader 1 | Sing the praises of our ancestors, those famous people who lived long ago. |
| Reader 2 | Some of them were kings or were famous for their courage. |
| Reader 3 | Some gave wise advice or spoke messages from God. |
| Reader 4 | There were leaders who made good decisions, who learned the wisdom passed down by our people, and who taught it to others. |
| Reader 1 | Some of our ancestors wrote poetry or music; |
| Reader 2 | others were rich and powerful, but lived in peace. |
| Readers 1-4 | We will praise these godly ones, whose righteous deeds have never been forgotten. |
| Reader 3 | Their good name has been handed down from generation to generation. |
| Reader 4 | Their families will live on, and each new generation will honor these ancestors. |

| | |
|---|---|
| Leader: | Lord of all, we praise your love for us and your gifts to us. We come before you full of gratitude for all those who have shown us your way. Hear our prayer as we say: We praise you and bless you, O Lord. |
| All | We praise you and bless you, O Lord. |

## Intercessions

| | |
|---|---|
| Pre-K | Thank you for our moms and dads. |
| All | We praise you and bless you, O Lord. |
| K | Thank you for their moms and dads. |
| All | We praise you and bless you, O Lord. |
| Grade 1 | Thank you for our brothers and sisters. |
| All | We praise you and bless you, O Lord. |
| Grade 2 | Thank you for our families. |
| All | We praise you and bless you, O Lord. |
| Grade 3 | Thank you for our friends. |
| All | We praise you and bless you, O Lord. |
| Grade 4 | Thank you for our teachers. |
| All | We praise you and bless you, O Lord. |
| Grade 5 | Thank you for all those who lead our country. |
| All | We praise you and bless you, O Lord. |
| Grade 6 | Thank you for all who guide us in faith. |
| All | We praise you and bless you, O Lord. |
| Grade 7 | Thank you for all your saints in heaven. |
| All | We praise you and bless you, O Lord. |
| Grade 8 | Thank you for all your saints on earth. |
| All | We praise you and bless you, O Lord. |

| | |
|---|---|
| Leader | Dear Lord, we praise you and bless you for your constant care for us. Keep us all holy and blameless in your sight, so that all will know of your greatness through us. Help us to be good disciples. |
| All | Amen. |

# Rejoice and Be Glad! Jesus Is Coming!

**Advent**

This prayer service is designed to help the children enjoy their anticipation and excitement, while at the same time offering reasons to rejoice that aren't focused on tons of gifts!

**Call to Prayer**

| Leader | In the name of the Father, and of the Son, and of the Holy Spirit. |
|---|---|
| All | Amen. |
| Leader | We gather today to celebrate the holy season of Advent, a time when we wait for the coming of Jesus into our midst. As Jesus was born of Mary, so can Jesus be born in each of our hearts if we open our minds and hearts to receive him, now and forever. Let us listen to the prophet Zephaniah. |

| **Reading** | **Zephaniah 3:14–18a** |
|---|---|
| Reader 1 | Sing aloud! Rejoice and exult with all your heart! |
| Reader 2 | The Lord has taken away the judgments against you. |
| Readers 1-4 | The Lord is in your midst; you shall fear disaster no more. |
| Reader 3 | On that day it shall be said: |
| Reader 4 | Do not fear; |
| Reader 1 | do not let your hands grow weak. |
| Readers 1-4 | The Lord, your God, is in your midst. |
| Reader 2 | He will rejoice over you with gladness, |
| Reader 3 | he will renew you in his love; |
| Reader 4 | he will exult over you with loud singing. |
| Readers 1-4 | The Lord, your God, is in your midst. |

| Leader | What strong and powerful words Zephaniah offers us about the goodness and mercy of our God. Let us praise God's wonderful work among us as we say: We rejoice with all our hearts. |
|---|---|
| All | We rejoice with all our hearts. |

## Intercessions

| | |
|---|---|
| Pre-K | We are happy you are with us. |
| All | We rejoice with all our hearts. |
| K | We are happy that you love us. |
| All | We rejoice with all our hearts. |
| Grade 1 | We are happy that we know you. |
| All | We rejoice with all our hearts. |
| Grade 2 | We are happy that we can praise you. |
| All | We rejoice with all our hearts. |
| Grade 3 | We are filled with joy at your goodness. |
| All | We rejoice with all our hearts. |
| Grade 4 | We are filled with joy at your mercy. |
| All | We rejoice with all our hearts. |
| Grade 5 | We are filled with joy at the world you have made. |
| All | We rejoice with all our hearts. |
| Grade 6 | We rejoice in all your gifts. |
| All | We rejoice with all our hearts. |
| Grade 7 | We rejoice in your comfort at sad times. |
| All | We rejoice with all our hearts. |
| Grade 8 | We rejoice in our power to do good works in your name. |
| All | We rejoice with all our hearts. |

| | |
|---|---|
| Leader | Lord of all, we eagerly await your coming into our hearts. Fill us with your Spirit that we may go forth and serve you. Light our path so we do not stumble, and show us where you need us most. We rejoice with all our hearts in this joyous season. Help us share your gifts with everyone we meet. |
| All | Amen. |

# Light of the World

**Christmas**

You probably won't get to use this one very often—perhaps the last day before vacation—but you might want to send it home so children can adapt for use during their Christmas holiday.

**Call to Prayer**

| | |
|---|---|
| Leader | In the name of the Father, and of the Son, and of the Holy Spirit. |
| All | Amen. |
| Leader | Christmas is such a busy time—we're shopping, we're dreaming, maybe we're packing, we're cleaning, we're hoping for a whole bundle of presents. Let's take a moment now in all this busyness to pray, and thank God for the immense gift of his Son, Jesus, whose birth we celebrate. How amazing is this gift? Let us listen to the words of the prophet Isaiah: |

**Reading**     Isaiah 9:2, 3, 6, 7

| | |
|---|---|
| Reader 1 | The people who walked in darkness have seen a great light; |
| Reader 2 | those who lived in a land of deep darkness—on them light has shined. |
| Reader 3 | You have multiplied the nation, you have increased its joy; |
| Reader 4 | they rejoice before you as with joy at the harvest. |
| Readers 1-4 | For a child has been born for us, |
| Reader 1 | a son given to us; |
| Reader 2 | Authority rests upon his shoulders; |
| Reader 3 | and he is named Wonderful Counselor, |
| Reader 4 | Mighty God, |
| Readers 1-2 | Everlasting Father, |
| Readers 3-4 | Prince of Peace. |
| Readers 1-4 | His authority shall grow continually, and there shall be endless peace. |
| | |
| Leader | Imagine God coming to live with us as a baby, to grow up just as we do, to eat and drink and play. Let us praise all God's gifts to us by saying: The Lord has given us light. |
| All: | The Lord has given us light. |

**Intercessions**

| | |
|---|---|
| Pre-K | Dear Lord, thank you for the light of life. |
| All | The Lord has given us light. |
| K | Dear Lord, thank you for the light of play. |
| All | The Lord has given us light. |
| Grade 1 | Dear Lord, thank you for the light of family. |
| All | The Lord has given us light. |
| Grade 2 | Dear Lord, thank you for the light of faith. |
| All | The Lord has given us light. |
| Grade 3 | Dear Lord, thank you for the light of welcome. |
| All | The Lord has given us light. |
| Grade 4 | Dear Lord, thank you for the light of hope. |
| All | The Lord has given us light. |
| Grade 5 | Dear Lord, thank you for the light of justice. |
| All | The Lord has given us light. |
| Grade 6 | Dear Lord, thank you for the light of learning. |
| All | The Lord has given us light. |
| Grade 7 | Dear Lord, thank you for the light of joy. |
| All | The Lord has given us light. |
| Grade 8 | Dear Lord, thank you for the light of peace. |
| All | The Lord has given us light. |

| | |
|---|---|
| Leader | God of all goodness, thank you for the light you have sent us in Jesus. As the shepherds recognized him in the face of a baby, let us recognize and welcome him in the faces of all we meet, neighbor and stranger alike. Keep us holy and blameless in your sight, and let your light guide us always. |
| All | Amen. |

# Seeing the Lord Face to Face

## Epiphany

Chances are you'll be back to school by now, and the children will still be a little distracted from their vacation. Why not take the time for a little "twelfth night" celebratory prayer to remind them of the joy of finding God everywhere?

## Call to Prayer

| | |
|---|---|
| Leader | In the name of the Father, and of the Son, and of the Holy Spirit. |
| All | Amen. |
| Leader | Lord, we gather here to sing of Christmas wonder one more time. On this wonderful day, we celebrate how your majesty and wonder were revealed to three wise people who represented the whole world. They came, they saw, and they believed. How can we do the same? Let us listen to the words of the apostle Paul. |

## Reading    Ephesians 1:3–6, 15–18

| | |
|---|---|
| Reader 1 | Blessed be the God and Father of our Lord Jesus Christ, who has blessed us in Christ with every spiritual blessing in the heavenly places, |
| Reader 2 | just as he chose us in Christ before the foundation of the world to be holy and blameless before him in love. |
| Reader 3 | He destined us for adoption as his children through Jesus Christ, according to the good pleasure of his will, |
| Reader 4 | to the praise of his glorious grace that he freely bestowed on us in the Beloved. |
| Reader 1 | I have heard of your faith in the Lord Jesus and your love towards all the saints, and for this reason I do not cease to give thanks for you as I remember you in my prayers. |
| Reader 2 | I pray that the God of our Lord Jesus Christ, the Father of glory, may give you a spirit of wisdom and revelation as you come to know him, |
| Reader 3 | so that, with the eyes of your heart enlightened, you may know what is the hope to which he has called you, |
| Reader 4 | what are the riches of his glorious inheritance among the saints. |
| Leader: | As we celebrate this wonderful gift of God and seek to do God's will, let us respond: Enlighten the eyes of our hearts. |
| All | Enlighten the eyes of our hearts. |

**Intercessions**

| | |
|---|---|
| Pre-K | Help us see you on the playground. |
| All | Enlighten the eyes of our hearts. |
| K | Help us see you in our teachers. |
| All | Enlighten the eyes of our hearts. |
| Grade 1 | Help us see you in our families. |
| All | Enlighten the eyes of our hearts. |
| Grade 2 | Help us see you in our parish. |
| All | Enlighten the eyes of our hearts. |
| Grade 3 | Help us see you in our neighborhoods. |
| All | Enlighten the eyes of our hearts. |
| Grade 4 | Help us see you in our soup kitchens. |
| All | Enlighten the eyes of our hearts. |
| Grade 5 | Help us see you in our shelters. |
| All | Enlighten the eyes of our hearts. |
| Grade 6 | Help us see you in our government. |
| All | Enlighten the eyes of our hearts. |
| Grade 7 | Help us see you in our world. |
| All | Enlighten the eyes of our hearts. |
| Grade 8 | Help us see you in each other. |
| All | Enlighten the eyes of our hearts. |

| | |
|---|---|
| Leader | Lord, you give us the grace to know you. Give us, too, the grace to see you everywhere and in everyone. May we bring your glorious message of hope, love, and peace to all. Transform us as you transformed the wise men, and give us the strength to spread your good news. |
| All | Amen. |

 # Creating Clean Hearts

**Ash Wednesday**

Lent is so much more than "giving up" things, though this is the dimension of the season that resonates most with little ones. By centering their focus on God's great gifts, especially the gift of forgiveness, you can make this a profoundly different and significant Lent.

**Call to Prayer**

| | |
|---|---|
| Leader | In the name of the Father, and of the Son, and of the Holy Spirit. |
| All | Amen. |
| Leader | We stand on the threshold of a forty-day journey. Our journey through the desert of Lent needs God's help and God's light. Let us pray today for the wisdom and grace to make this Lent a truly blessed season, so that we may join our praises with those who will be baptized and confirmed and receive Eucharist for the first time at the Easter Vigil. We seek pure hearts and souls formed and ready for God's purpose, as Psalm 51 reminds us. |

**Reading**      **Psalm 51:1–4, 10–13, 15**

| | |
|---|---|
| Reader 1 | Have mercy on me, O God, according to your steadfast love, |
| Reader 2 | according to your abundant mercy, blot out my transgressions. |
| Readers 1-4 | Wash me thoroughly from my iniquity, and cleanse me from my sin. |
| Reader 3 | For I know my transgressions, |
| Reader 4 | and my sin is ever before me. |
| Readers 1-4 | Against you, you alone, have I sinned, and done what is evil in your sight. |
| Reader 1 | Create in me a clean heart, O God, and put a new and right spirit within me. |
| Reader 2 | Do not cast me away from your presence, and do not take your holy spirit from me. |
| Reader 3 | Restore to me the joy of your salvation, and sustain in me a willing spirit. |
| Reader 4 | Then I will teach transgressors your ways, and sinners will return to you. |
| Readers 1-4 | O Lord, open my lips, and my mouth will declare your praise. |
| | |
| Leader | Dear Lord, we come to you humbly and with contrite hearts. Purify our hearts and minds so that we may joyfully reflect your light and love. Hear us as we pray: Let us sing your praise. |
| All | Let us sing your praise. |

**Intercessions**

| | |
|---|---|
| Pre-K | Lord, thank you for forgiving us when we get mad at others. |
| All | Let us sing your praise. |
| K | Lord, thank you for being with us when we're sad. |
| All | Let us sing your praise. |
| Grade 1 | Lord, thank you for listening when we need to talk. |
| All | Let us sing your praise. |
| Grade 2 | Lord, thank you for comforting us when we're afraid. |
| All | Let us sing your praise. |
| Grade 3 | Lord, thank you for giving us your Spirit. |
| All | Let us sing your praise. |
| Grade 4 | Lord, thank you for giving us your Son. |
| All | Let us sing your praise. |
| Grade 5 | Lord, thank you for being patient when we fail. |
| All | Let us sing your praise. |
| Grade 6 | Lord, thank you for being strong when we are weak. |
| All | Let us sing your praise. |
| Grade 7 | Lord, thank you for giving us the faith to praise you. |
| All | Let us sing your praise. |
| Grade 8 | Lord, thank you for the gift of seeing you in others. |
| All | Let us sing your praise. |

| | |
|---|---|
| Leader | Lord, heal us and wash us clean of sin. Purify us that we may be bright and shining witnesses of your love. Let us join in prayer for all those who will join the church at Easter, that their faith, too, may never be shaken. Guide us in your love that we may serve you well, all through Lent and always. |
| All | Amen. |

 # God Is for Us!

**Lent**

Lent seems to go on forever for children, but because it is such a special time in the church year, it's an ideal time to reinforce rituals with them. This prayer service has been designed to be used throughout Lent, to help remind children of the gift of baptism that some of the parish community will be receiving—and that all of us will be renewing—at the Easter Vigil.

**Call to Prayer**

| | |
|---|---|
| Leader | In the name of the Father, and of the Son, and of the Holy Spirit. |
| All | Amen. |
| Leader | Dear Lord, as we journey through these forty days, we ask your blessings on those of our parish community who will be welcomed into the faith at Easter. Help us to be examples for them, and to realize that we have as much to learn from them as they do from us. Let us listen to the words of the apostle Paul to the Romans: |

**Reading**     **Romans 8:31b–34**

| | |
|---|---|
| Reader 1 | If God is for us, who is against us? |
| Reader 2 | He who did not withhold his own Son, but gave him up for all of us, will he not with him also give us everything else? |
| Reader 3 | Who will bring any charge against God's elect? It is God who justifies. |
| Reader 4 | Who is to condemn? It is Christ Jesus, who died, yes, who was raised, who is at the right hand of God, who indeed intercedes for us. |
| | |
| Leader | Dear Lord, we can never thank you enough for the great gift of your Son, who brings us close to you. We want to share this good news with others. Stand by our side and defend us as we proclaim your glory. Hear us as we pray: If God is for us, who is against us? |
| All | If God is for us, who is against us? |

**Intercessions**

| | |
|---|---|
| Pre-K | God is on our side. |
| All | If God is for us, who is against us? |
| K | God is with us always. |
| All | If God is for us, who is against us? |
| Grade 1 | God is with us in all that we do. |
| All | If God is for us, who is against us? |
| Grade 2 | God is with us in all the people we meet. |
| All | If God is for us, who is against us? |
| Grade 3 | God is with us at Mass and in Communion. |
| All | If God is for us, who is against us? |
| Grade 4 | God is with us when we are sorry for our sins. |
| All | If God is for us, who is against us? |
| Grade 5 | God is with us always and everywhere. |
| All | If God is for us, who is against us? |
| Grade 6 | God is with us in our parish, our homes, and our community. |
| All | If God is for us, who is against us? |
| Grade 7 | God is with us and with all who seek to know his Good News. |
| All | If God is for us, who is against us? |
| Grade 8 | God is with us in the miracle of dying and rising. |
| All | If God is for us, who is against us? |
| | |
| Leader | Dear Lord, we praise your glory and your presence among us. Help us to welcome all who want to share in your Good News. Help us always to be examples of your love. Keep us holy in your sight. |
| All | Amen. |

# Give Thanks to the Lord!

**Easter**

This prayer service has been designed to be used throughout the Easter season, to remind everyone of the glorious promise revealed and fulfilled in the resurrection.

**Call to Prayer**

| | |
|---|---|
| Leader | In the name of the Father, and of the Son, and of the Holy Spirit. |
| All | Amen. |
| Leader | Dear Lord, we rejoice in the miracle of the resurrection. We rejoice in this season of new life and new hope. We rejoice as the psalmist did long ago. |

**Reading**   **Psalm 105:1–2, 3–4, 6–7, 8–9**

| | |
|---|---|
| Reader 1 | O give thanks to the Lord, call on his name, |
| Reader 2 | Make known his deeds among the peoples. |
| Reader 3 | Sing to him, sing praises to him; |
| Readers 1-4 | tell of all his wonderful works. |
| Reader 4 | Glory in his holy name, |
| Reader 1 | Let the hearts of those who seek the Lord rejoice. |
| Reader 2 | Seek the Lord and his strength; |
| Reader 3 | Seek his presence continually. |
| Reader 4 | O offspring of his servant Abraham, children of Jacob, his chosen ones. |
| Readers 1-4 | The Lord is our God, bringing judgment everywhere on earth. |
| Readers 1-2 | He is mindful of his covenant for ever, |
| Readers 3-4 | of the word that he commanded, for a thousand generations, |
| Readers 1-4 | the covenant that he made with Abraham, his sworn promise to Isaac. |
| | |
| Leader | Dear Lord, we gather to celebrate your goodness, your care, and your love. You have forgiven our faults. We are grateful for your gentleness and mercy. Hear us as we pray: Give thanks to the Lord. |
| All | Give thanks to the Lord. |

## Intercessions

| | |
|---|---|
| Pre-K | Thank you, God, for our family. |
| All | Give thanks to the Lord. |
| K | Thank you, God, for our homes. |
| All | Give thanks to the Lord. |
| Grade 1 | Thank you, God, for our friends. |
| All | Give thanks to the Lord. |
| Grade 2 | Thank you, God, for our teachers. |
| All | Give thanks to the Lord. |
| Grade 3 | Thank you, God, for the chance to praise you. |
| All | Give thanks to the Lord. |
| Grade 4 | Thank you, God, for the gift of your Son. |
| All | Give thanks to the Lord. |
| Grade 5 | Thank you, God, for making us your children. |
| All | Give thanks to the Lord. |
| Grade 6 | Thank you, God, for sending us your Spirit. |
| All | Give thanks to the Lord. |
| Grade 7 | Thank you, God, for all your wonderful works. |
| All | Give thanks to the Lord. |
| Grade 8 | Thank you, God, for the gift of faith. |
| All | Give thanks to the Lord. |
| | |
| Leader | Dear Lord, we praise you and we thank you in all we say and do. Help us to spread the joy of your goodness to everyone we meet, so that everyone will come to know how glorious you are. We ask this in Jesus' name. |
| All | Amen. |

 # Send Us Your Spirit

**Pentecost**

As you prepare to send the school community off for summer vacation, this is a great opportunity to remind them of their call to be disciples each and every day.

**Call to Prayer**

| | |
|---|---|
| Leader | Lord, send out your Spirit. |
| All | And renew the face of the earth. |
| Leader | Dear Lord, our fifty days of rejoicing have prepared us to go forth and carry your Good News to others. You have kept all of your promises. You have sent your Spirit to us to guide us in your ways. We rejoice to hear the story again. |

**Reading**    Acts 2:1–11

| | |
|---|---|
| Reader 1 | When the day of Pentecost had come, they were all together in one place. |
| Reader 2 | And suddenly from heaven there came a sound like the rush of a violent wind, and it filled the entire house where they were sitting. |
| Reader 3 | Divided tongues, as of fire, appeared among them, and a tongue rested on each of them. |
| Reader 4 | All of them were filled with the Holy Spirit and began to speak in other languages, as the Spirit gave them ability. |
| Reader 1 | Now there were devout Jews from every nation under heaven living in Jerusalem. |
| Reader 2 | And at this sound the crowd gathered and was bewildered, because each one heard them speaking in the native language of each. |
| Reader 3 | Amazed and astonished, they asked, |
| Reader 4 | "Are not all these who are speaking Galileans? And how is it that we hear them speaking about God's deeds of power, each of us, in our own native language?" |
| Leader | Dear Lord, we live in difficult times, when people do not speak to one another; when they find it easier to disagree than to find ways to work together. Send your Spirit to us that we may make your Good News heard and understood throughout our school, community, and world. Hear us as we pray: Send us your Spirit. |
| All | Send us your Spirit. |

## Intercessions

| | |
|---|---|
| Pre-K | With your Spirit we can make friends. |
| All | Send us your Spirit. |
| K | With your Spirit we can work hard. |
| All | Send us your Spirit. |
| Grade 1 | With your Spirit we can have courage to do what is right. |
| All | Send us your Spirit. |
| Grade 2 | With your Spirit we can try to heal hurts. |
| All | Send us your Spirit. |
| Grade 3 | With your Spirit we can try to be peacemakers. |
| All | Send us your Spirit. |
| Grade 4 | With your Spirit we can try to break down barriers and build bridges. |
| All | Send us your Spirit. |
| Grade 5 | With your Spirit we can challenge ourselves to grow. |
| All | Send us your Spirit. |
| Grade 6 | With your Spirit we can use our gifts to your greater glory. |
| All | Send us your Spirit. |
| Grade 7 | With your Spirit we can teach others about your love. |
| All | Send us your Spirit. |
| Grade 8 | With your Spirit we can  work for understanding and peace among all who are filled with conflict. |
| All | Send us your Spirit. |
| | |
| Leader | Dear Lord, we seek to be understood by all your children, as your disciples were on that day when your Spirit descended upon them. Help us keep our goals clear, our vision steady and sure, and our hearts and minds turned always to you. We ask this through Jesus, your Son. |
| All | Amen. |

#  In Honor of Mary

**Marian feasts**

This prayer was originally written as a May Crowning service, but it could be used equally well—with some adaptation, of course—to celebrate Mary's birthday on September 8, the Immaculate Conception on December 8, or the Annunciation on March 25.

**Call to Prayer**

| | |
|---|---|
| Leader | In the name of the Father, and of the Son, and of the Holy Spirit. |
| All | Amen. |
| Leader | We gather today to celebrate Mary, Mother of God, Mother of the Church, and Mother of us all. Let us lift our voices in praise and prayer as she did with her cousin, Elizabeth. |

**Reading    Luke 1:48–56 (CEV)**

| | |
|---|---|
| Reader 1 | With all my heart I praise the Lord, and I am glad because of God my Savior. He cares for me, his humble servant. From now on, all people will say God has blessed me. |
| Reader 2 | God All-Powerful has done great things for me, and his name is holy. He always shows mercy to everyone who worships him. |
| Reader 3 | The Lord has used his powerful arm to scatter those who are proud. He drags strong rulers from their thrones and puts humble people in places of power. |
| Reader 4 | He gives the hungry good things to eat, and he sends the rich away with nothing in their hands. He helps his servant Israel and is always merciful to his people. He made this promise to our ancestors, to Abraham and his family forever! |
| Leader: | Mary is the first and greatest disciple. She carried Jesus within her, she watched him as he grew, and she cradled him again in her arms when he was taken down from the cross. She waited with the apostles and received, as they did, the glorious gift of the Holy Spirit at Pentecost. We celebrate her today for her goodness, her unwavering faith, and her constant concern for us. Let us call on her now with some of her wonderful names, as we pray: Keep us in your care. |
| All | Keep us in your care. |

**Intercessions**

| | |
|---|---|
| Pre-K | Mary, Star of the Sea |
| All | Keep us in your care. |
| K | Mary, the Morning Star |
| All | Keep us in your care. |
| Grade 1 | Mary, Cause of our Joy |
| All | Keep us in your care. |
| Grade 2 | Mary, Mirror of Justice |
| All | Keep us in your care. |
| Grade 3 | Mary, Refuge in Time of Danger |
| All | Keep us in your care. |
| Grade 4 | Mary, Woman Clothed with the Sun |
| All | Keep us in your care. |
| Grade 5 | Mary, Queen of Peace |
| All | Keep us in your care. |
| Grade 6 | Mary, Queen of Creation |
| All | Keep us in your care. |
| Grade 7 | Mary, Queen of all Saints |
| All | Keep us in your care. |
| Grade 8 | Mary, Queen of Heaven and Earth |
| All | Keep us in your care. |

Leader    [Here the crowning of the statue of Mary could take place, with the singing of an appropriate Marian hymn.]

Lord of all, we praise you for your countless gifts. Most of all, today we praise you for Mary, whom you chose to be the mother of your Son. Help us follow her example of discipleship, and keep us holy in your sight. We ask this through Jesus Christ, your Son, our Lord.

All    Amen.

# Sacraments

One of the most important things we ever do is accompany our children on their journey of Christian initiation. Unfortunately, this is sometimes done in isolation rather than involving the entire school community. These prayer services are designed to get everyone involved in praying for and blessing those who are about to celebrate sacraments for the first time.

# Thank You for Your Goodness

**For those preparing for First Penance**

**Call to Prayer**

| | |
|---|---|
| Leader | In the name of the Father, and of the Son, and of the Holy Spirit. |
| All | Amen. |
| Leader | We gather today to rejoice with the children who will shortly be celebrating the sacrament of First Penance. May our prayer rise with theirs, so that God will hear our wonderful song of praise for this great gift. |

**Reading**     **Luke 18:15–17**

| | |
|---|---|
| Reader 1 | People were bringing even infants to Jesus that he might touch them. |
| Reader 2 | When the disciples saw it, they sternly ordered them not to do it. |
| Reader 3 | But Jesus called for them and said, |
| Reader 4 | "Let the little children come to me, and do not stop them; for it is to such as these that the kingdom of God belongs. |
| Readers 1-4 | Truly I tell you, whoever does not receive the kingdom of God as a little child will never enter it." |

| | |
|---|---|
| Leader | Dear Lord, we come before you in wonder and awe at the many gifts you give us. Soon our (number) graders will be receiving your gift of forgiveness. Open their eyes to see how often and in how many ways this gift is shown around them. Help them share this gift with everyone they know. Hear us now as we pray: Thank you for your goodness, Lord. |
| All | Thank you for your goodness, Lord. |

**Intercessions**

| | |
|---|---|
| Pre-K | For our families who love us and forgive us. |
| All | Thank you for your goodness, Lord. |
| K | For our friends who love us and forgive us. |
| All | Thank you for your goodness, Lord. |
| Grade 1 | For those we don't like who love us and forgive us. |
| All | Thank you for your goodness, Lord. |
| Grade 2 | For people in our neighborhood who love us and forgive us. |
| All | Thank you for your goodness, Lord. |
| Grade 3 | For our teachers who love us and forgive us. |
| All | Thank you for your goodness, Lord. |
| Grade 4 | For all those in our families whom we need to forgive. |
| All | Thank you for your goodness, Lord. |
| Grade 5 | For all of our friends whom we need to forgive. |
| All | Thank you for your goodness, Lord. |
| Grade 6 | For all those we know whom we need to forgive. |
| All | Thank you for your goodness, Lord. |
| Grade 7 | For everyone who reveals your goodness to us. |
| All | Thank you for your goodness, Lord. |
| Grade 8 | For those about to receive your forgiveness, who remind us of our call to forgive. |
| All | Thank you for your goodness, Lord. |

| | |
|---|---|
| Leader | Dear Lord, we thank you for your goodness in being with us in all that we do. Help us see your forgiveness in all those around us who touch our days. Open our eyes and ears and hearts to respond in kindness and mercy to all who seek our forgiveness. And bless these children, holy and blameless in your sight. May they always be strong witnesses of your love and compassion now and forever. |
| All | Amen. |

 # May God Bless You Always

**For those preparing for First Eucharist**

This can be a time of great rejoicing throughout the school—welcoming the children into full communion in the faith. This prayer service is also designed for those children of catechetical age who may be entering the church family at the Easter Vigil.

**Call to Prayer**

| | |
|---|---|
| Leader | In the name of the Father, and of the Son, and of the Holy Spirit. |
| All | Amen. |
| Leader | We gather today to rejoice with those of us who are about to receive Jesus for the first time in Eucharist. They have practiced, they have studied, and we know how eager they are to join in the holy communion of our church. They stand on a new threshold of discipleship. Let us celebrate their new role! |

**Reading**   **1 Peter 2:4–5, 9–10**

| | |
|---|---|
| Reader 1 | Come to him, a living stone, |
| Reader 2 | though rejected by mortals yet chosen and precious in God's sight; |
| Reader 3 | Like living stones, let yourselves be built into a spiritual house, |
| Reader 1 | to be a holy priesthood, |
| Reader 2 | to offer spiritual sacrifices acceptable to God through Jesus Christ. |
| Readers 1-4 | You are a chosen race, a royal priesthood, a holy nation, God's own people, in order that you may proclaim the mighty acts of him who called you out of darkness into his marvelous light. |
| Reader 3 | Once you were not a people, but now you are God's people. |
| Reader 4 | Once you had not received mercy, but now you have received mercy. |
| | |
| Leader: | God of all goodness and love, we thank you for all your blessings. Be with us now as we gather to bless those among us who are about to celebrate First Eucharist. Be with them as they come happily to receive you. Hear us as we pray for them: May God bless you always. |
| All | May God bless you always. |

## Intercessions

| | |
|---|---|
| Pre-K | As you work and play |
| All | May God bless you always. |
| K | As you study and pray |
| All | May God bless you always. |
| Grade 1 | As you learn and grow |
| All | May God bless you always. |
| Grade 2 | As you reach out in love |
| All | May God bless you always. |
| Grade 3 | As you join in communion |
| All | May God bless you always. |
| Grade 4 | As you share your joy with us |
| All | May God bless you always. |
| Grade 5 | As you come back to school, changed but the same |
| All | May God bless you always. |
| Grade 6 | As you learn more and more |
| All | May God bless you always. |
| Grade 7 | As you achieve greater and greater things in life |
| All | May God bless you always. |
| Grade 8 | As you teach your own families about God's great love |
| All | May God bless you always. |

| | |
|---|---|
| Leader | Good and gracious God, our children are ready and eager to receive you, to take their prepared place within our church family. Bless them today and always in your infinite mercy and love. We ask all this in the name of your Son, our savior, Jesus. |
| All | Amen. |

# Fill Them with Your Spirit

**For those preparing for Confirmation**

This prayer service is designed with intercessions that are not specifically grade-oriented, so that any groups in a high school or religious education program can take part. This could even be used at a parish gathering to celebrate the young people. Note: the Scripture reading has been adapted to reflect all those celebrating the sacrament.

## Call to Prayer

| | |
|---|---|
| Leader | In the name of the Father, and of the Son, and of the Holy Spirit. |
| All | Amen. |
| Leader | We gather today in celebration of our young people who are about to be confirmed. They have looked to us for guidance; with this sacrament they begin to take their own places as examples of wisdom and living faith. Listen to the words of God's call. |

## Reading    Isaiah 42:1–3, 6–7, 10

| | |
|---|---|
| Reader 1 | Here are my servants, whom I uphold, my chosen, in whom my soul delights. |
| Reader 2 | I have put my spirit upon them; they will bring forth justice to the nations. |
| Reader 3 | They will not cry or lift their voices, or make them heard in the street. |
| Reader 4 | A bruised reed they will not break, and a dimly burning wick they will not quench. |
| Reader 1 | They will faithfully bring forth justice. |
| Reader 2 | I am the Lord, I have called you in righteousness, I have taken you by the hand and kept you; |
| Reader 3 | I have given you as a covenant to the people, a light to the nations, |
| Reader 4 | to open the eyes that are blind, to bring out prisoners from the dungeon. |
| Readers 1-4 | Sing to the Lord a new song, his praise from the end of the earth! |
| | |
| Leader | Praise to you, Lord, for these young people, newly formed disciples. Through their study and their work in our community, they have become aware of what discipleship entails. Make them ever and always aware of the gifts of your Spirit, that they may be sure and confident witnesses of your love. Hear us as we pray: Fill them with your Spirit, Lord. |
| All | Fill them with your Spirit, Lord. |

## Intercessions

| | |
|---|---|
| Reader | Let your love and joy surround them and radiate out to all they meet. |
| All | Fill them with your Spirit, Lord. |
| Reader | Let your peace surround them and become their watchword in all they do. |
| All | Fill them with your Spirit, Lord. |
| Reader | Let your patience and kindness fill them and be the arms that they offer to others. |
| All | Fill them with your Spirit, Lord. |
| Reader | Let your generosity enfold them in a garment big enough to be shared without thought or doubt. |
| All | Fill them with your Spirit, Lord. |
| Reader | Let your faithfulness to them be clearly evident in the faith that they proclaim to others. |
| All | Fill them with your Spirit, Lord. |
| Reader | Let your gentleness be their first response to any cry for help. |
| All | Fill them with your Spirit, Lord. |
| Reader | Let your self-control guide them in lives of holiness. |
| All | Fill them with your Spirit, Lord. |
| Reader | Let their lives be always guided by your Spirit. |
| All | Fill them with your Spirit, Lord. |
| | |
| Leader | Lord, we praise your goodness, your mercy, your love. You have given us such amazing gifts in these young people. Help them share their vision and conviction with everyone they meet, in all that they do, so that they will always give you glory. We ask this through the goodness of your Son, our savior, Jesus. |
| All | Amen. |

# Celebrations

You are sure to find many other reasons to gather to celebrate during the course of the year. Here you will find selections for Thanksgiving, Martin Luther King/World Peace Day, Graduation, and a couple of prayer services for teachers—who can always use our prayers!

# In Praise and Thanksgiving

## Thanksgiving

Before the Thanksgiving break, it would be wonderful to assemble the school to offer thanks for all of God's blessings.

## Call to Prayer

| | |
|---|---|
| Leader | In the name of the Father, and of the Son, and of the Holy Spirit. |
| All | Amen. |
| Leader | We gather today to celebrate the goodness of our God. Each of you is a reflection of God's face, a witness of God's love. As our country prepares to offer a day of thanksgiving, let us offer our own thanks and praise to our wonderful God. |

## Reading      Psalm 147:1, 4–8, 11, 14

| | |
|---|---|
| Readers 1-4 | Praise the Lord! |
| Reader 1 | How good it is to sing praises to our God; for he is gracious, and a song of praise is fitting. |
| Reader 2 | He determines the number of the the stars; he gives to all of them their names. |
| Reader 3 | Great is our Lord, and abundant in power; his understanding is beyond measure. |
| Reader 4 | The Lord lifts up the downtrodden; he casts the wicked to the ground. |
| Readers 1-4 | Praise the Lord! |
| Reader 1 | Sing to the Lord with thanksgiving; make melody to our God on the lyre. |
| Reader 2 | He covers the heavens with clouds, prepares rain for the earth, makes grass grow on the hills. |
| Reader 3 | The Lord takes pleasure in those who worship him, in those who hope in his steadfast love. |
| Reader 4 | He grants peace within your borders; he fills you with the finest of wheat. |
| Readers 1-4 | Praise the Lord! |
| | |
| Leader | Dear Lord, your works surround us daily. Help us recognize you in the fallen leaves, the rivers and seas, the mountains and valleys, all living creatures, the shelter of our homes, and the warmth of our care for one another. Hear us as we pray: Praise the Lord! |
| All | Praise the Lord! |

**Intercessions**

| | |
|---|---|
| Pre-K | For all good things to eat |
| All | Praise the Lord! |
| K | For all good things to play with |
| All | Praise the Lord! |
| Grade 1 | For all good things to read |
| All | Praise the Lord! |
| Grade 2 | For all our friends |
| All | Praise the Lord! |
| Grade 3 | For all our teachers |
| All | Praise the Lord! |
| Grade 4 | For all our families |
| All | Praise the Lord! |
| Grade 5 | For our pastor and our parish |
| All | Praise the Lord! |
| Grade 6 | For our homes and neighborhoods |
| All | Praise the Lord! |
| Grade 7 | For our country and our world |
| All | Praise the Lord! |
| Grade 8 | For one another and for God's ever-present love |
| All | Praise the Lord! |

| | |
|---|---|
| Leader | Lord, we praise you for your goodness. Yet sometimes we find it hard to see or grasp this goodness. Help us remember that you are always with us, in the darkness as well as the light. Keep us holy in your sight, and let our voices always be raised to you in praise and thanksgiving. |
| All | Amen. |

# Let There Be Peace

**Martin Luther King/World Peace Day**

This prayer service could be used on either of the days indicated, or at any time when it would be good to gather and pray for peace—at school, in the neighborhood, or in the world.

**Call to Prayer**

| | |
|---|---|
| Leader | In the name of the Father, and of the Son, and of the Holy Spirit. |
| All | Amen. |
| Leader | We gather today to celebrate peace, the peace of Christ, the peace that God offers us. Often in our war-torn world, peace seems very far away, a dim possibility. But God has promised us peace. Let us raise our voices in the hope that it will come soon and will fulfill the message of all God's prophets of peace. |

**Reading**     Isaiah 32:15–18

| | |
|---|---|
| Reader 1 | A spirit from on high is poured out on us,<br>and the wilderness becomes a fruitful field. |
| Reader 2 | Then justice will dwell in the wilderness,<br>and righteousness abide in the fruitful field. |
| Reader 3 | The effect of righteousness will be peace,<br>and the result of righteousness, quietness and trust forever. |
| Reader 4 | My people will abide in a peaceful habitation,<br>in secure dwellings, and in quiet resting-places. |
| Readers 1-4 | A spirit from on high is poured out on us,<br>and the wilderness becomes a fruitful field. |
| Leader | God of all goodness and light, we seek you in the darkness of our world. Your prophets have spoken of peace, your people have sought it and worked for it for generations. Help us make peace a reality in our time, in this place, and in our world. Hear us as we pray: Lord, send down your Spirit. |
| All | Lord, send down your Spirit. |

## Intercessions

| | |
|---|---|
| Pre-K | Help us know what is right and do it. |
| All | Lord, send down your Spirit. |
| K | Help us find you in everyone we meet. |
| All | Lord, send down your Spirit. |
| Grade 1 | Help us hear your messengers of good news. |
| All | Lord, send down your Spirit. |
| Grade 2 | Help us be messengers of good news. |
| All | Lord, send down your Spirit. |
| Grade 3 | When we are frightened, help us remember your words of peace. |
| All | Lord, send down your Spirit. |
| Grade 4 | When we are hopeful, help us kindle that hope in others. |
| All | Lord, send down your Spirit. |
| Grade 5 | When we are wronged, help us seek justice instead of revenge. |
| All | Lord, send down your Spirit. |
| Grade 6 | Where we are quick to judge, make us quicker to understand. |
| All | Lord, send down your Spirit. |
| Grade 7 | Where we are quick to condemn, make us quicker to praise. |
| All | Lord, send down your Spirit. |
| Grade 8 | Where there is darkness, let us be light for others so your promise of peace will be known in our world. |
| All | Lord, send down your Spirit. |
| | |
| Leader | Lord of all, we want to help make your kingdom real in this place and in this time. Hear our voices raised with those of your prophets of all ages—Isaiah, Martin, Mohandas, Dorothy, Joseph, Oscar, and so many others. Help us follow their example, so that your peace will reign in our hearts and in our world. We ask this through our savior, your Son, Jesus. |
| All | Amen. |

# Keep Them in Your Heart

## Graduation

This can be a bittersweet time for your older students. They have enjoyed being the "big folk on campus"; at the same time that they know they are soon to be the "new kids on the block." This is a great opportunity to join the whole school community in prayer to offer love and support to the graduates.

## Call to Prayer

| | |
|---|---|
| Leader | In the name of the Father, and of the Son, and of the Holy Spirit. |
| All | Amen. |
| Leader | We gather today to celebrate our graduates, those whose faces have become so familiar, those who have gone from being new arrivals to role models. We will miss them, and we thank them for sharing their gifts with us. |

## Reading     Acts 1:6–11

| | |
|---|---|
| Reader 1 | When they had come together, the disciples asked Jesus, "Lord, is this the time when you will restore the kingdom to Israel?" |
| Reader 2 | He replied, "It is not for you to know the times or periods that the Father has set by his own authority. But you will receive power when the Holy Spirit has come upon you; and you will be my witnesses in Jerusalem, in all Judea and Samaria, and to the ends of the earth." |
| Reader 3 | When he had said this, as they were watching, he was lifted up, and a cloud took him out of their sight. While he was going and they were gazing up towards heaven, suddenly two men in white robes stood by them. |
| Reader 4 | They said, "Men of Galilee, why do you stand looking up towards heaven? This Jesus, who has been taken up from you into heaven, will come in the same way as you saw him go into heaven." |
| | |
| Leader | God of all goodness, we are sending our children out into your world. Help them, guide them, surround them with your Spirit, so that they may carry your message to all they meet as they journey through life. Hear us, Lord, as we pray: Keep them in your heart, Lord. |
| All | Keep them in your heart, Lord. |

**Intercessions**

| | |
|---|---|
| Pre-K | Make them holy and wise. |
| All | Keep them in your heart, Lord. |
| K | Make their hearts loving and kind. |
| All | Keep them in your heart, Lord. |
| Grade 1 | Make their roads easy to follow. |
| All | Keep them in your heart, Lord. |
| Grade 2 | Make their troubles small. |
| All | Keep them in your heart, Lord. |
| Grade 3 | Make their faith grow always stronger. |
| All | Keep them in your heart, Lord. |
| Grade 4 | Make their hearts burn with love for you and your children. |
| All | Keep them in your heart, Lord. |
| Grade 5 | May their lives be filled with blessings. |
| All | Keep them in your heart, Lord. |
| Grade 6 | May their hearts be full of courage. |
| All | Keep them in your heart, Lord. |
| Grade 7 | May we follow their example. |
| All | Keep them in your heart, Lord. |
| Grade 8 | May we always be at home here. |
| All | Keep them in your heart, Lord. |

Leader       Dear Lord, we have placed our petitions before you. Guide our young people in your service. Keep them always mindful of your great compassion and love, and give them the tools to spread your message to all they meet. Let them always consider this place their home. May our arms always be open to welcome them back to share the adventures they will discover. We ask all this, as we ask everything, through your Son, Jesus, our savior.

All       Amen.

# May God Be Praised for You

**Teacher Appreciation Day**

This prayer can be used during Catholic Schools Week, on Teacher Appreciation Day, with parents and children participating. It could easily be adapted to be a celebration of volunteers as well.

**Call to Prayer**

| | |
|---|---|
| Leader | In the name of the Father, and of the Son, and of the Holy Spirit. |
| All | Amen. |
| Leader | God Almighty, Lord of life, giver of all good, we praise you for your goodness, for your blessings, for your presence here with us in this holy place and at this holy time. Today we gather before you to praise and bless our teachers, those whose daily charge it is to help us impart to our children the wisdom and wonder of your world, the knowledge of your will, and the tools to do your will in their lives. We trust them with this task, knowing that their faith and hope come from you. In all ways, and every day, let our feelings echo the words of Paul to the Philippians: |

| **Reading** | **Philippians 1:3–11 (CEV)** |
|---|---|
| Reader 1 | Every time I think of you, I thank my God. And whenever I mention you in my prayers, it makes me happy. This is because you have taken part with me in spreading the good news from the first day you heard about it. |
| Reader 2 | God is the one who began this good work in you, and I am certain that he won't stop before it is complete on the day that Christ Jesus returns. You have a special place in my heart. |
| Reader 3 | My prayer is that your love may more and more abound, both in understanding and wealth of experience, so that with a clear conscience and blameless conduct you may learn to value the things that really matter, up to the very day of Christ. |
| Reader 4 | I pray that your love will keep on growing and that you will fully know and understand how to make the right choices. Then you will still be pure and innocent when Christ returns. |
| | |
| Leader | As we name the blessings our teachers bestow on us, let us respond: May God be praised for you. |
| All | May God be praised for you. |

## Intercessions

| | |
|---|---|
| Pre-K | You bless us when you teach us what you know and how to grow. |
| All | May God be praised for you. |
| K | You bless us with new things to learn, fun things to do, and friendship. |
| All | May God be praised for you. |
| Grade 1 | You bless us with attention, so we never feel left out. |
| All | May God be praised for you. |
| Grade 2 | You bless us with your trust so we can learn, create, and soar. |
| All | May God be praised for you. |
| Grade 3 | You bless us with the rules we need, the tools we use, and loving, constant caring. |
| All | May God be praised for you. |
| Grade 4 | You bless us with enthusiasm, discovery, and delight. |
| All | May God be praised for you. |
| Grade 5 | You bless us with your ears to hear, your gentleness, your help. |
| All | May God be praised for you. |
| Grade 6 | You bless us with new challenges, issues to face, and problems we can solve. |
| All | May God be praised for you. |
| Grade 7 | You bless us with excitement over newly seen horizons. You help us seek new heights there and discover whole new worlds. |
| All | May God be praised for you. |
| Grade 8 | You bless us with your time and talent, and wisdom shared with all. You bless us in all you do each day. |
| All | May God be praised for you. |

Leader    Dear God, you hear our hopes and dreams. Hear us now as we celebrate these wonderful teachers, and send your blessing upon them.

[Here the community may be invited to extend their hands in blessing over the teachers.]

Bless and sanctify these teachers as they continue in their sacred work of education, entrusting the wisdom of the ages and the knowledge of your love and will to us all. Hold them in your heart, refresh them when they tire, comfort them when they despair, and magnify their moments of joy and peace. Bless them as they bless us, and this small spot of earth will echo an unending hymn of praise. We ask this, as we ask everything, through Jesus Christ, our Lord.

All    Amen.

# Wisdom and Wonder in Our Midst

**Teacher Appreciation Day**

**Call to Prayer**

Leader    In the name of the Father, and of the Son, and of the Holy Spirit.

All    Amen.

Leader    We gather today with grateful hearts to celebrate our teachers. They help us to make our school holy ground, and to sanctify each moment of our days. May the knowledge they share in all different subjects and disciplines lead us to Wisdom, as Scripture depicts her:

**Reading**    **Wisdom 7:24—8:1 (CEV)**

Reader 1    Wisdom moves more easily than anything else and is so pure that she is everywhere at once.

Reader 2    Wisdom is the breath of God's power, the true reflection of the glory of God All-Powerful, so she cannot be touched by anything impure.

Reader 3    Wisdom is like a mirror reflecting the eternal light of God's deeds and goodness.

Reader 4    Though Wisdom is and remains only one being, she can do anything and she renews all things.

Reader 1    In each generation she enters the souls of the faithful, making them into prophets and friends of God,

Reader 2    since God's favorite people are those who live with her.

Reader 3    Wisdom is more beautiful than the sun and the stars.

Reader 4    She is far superior to daylight, because it turns to darkness, but she cannot be changed by the power of evil.

Readers 1-4    Wisdom rules the universe and keeps it in order.

Leader    Dear God, you have sent us these teachers and have granted each of them the grace and power to lead and inspire us. Hear us as we pray: We sing your praises, Lord.

All    We sing your praises, Lord.

**Intercessions**

| | |
|---|---|
| Pre-K | Thank you for these teachers who help us be your friends. |
| All | We sing your praises, Lord. |
| K | Thank you for these teachers who share your world with us. |
| All | We sing your praises, Lord. |
| Grade 1 | Thank you for these teachers who reflect your holy light. |
| All | We sing your praises, Lord. |
| Grade 2 | Thank you for these teachers who order all things well. |
| All | We sing your praises, Lord. |
| Grade 3 | Thank you for these teachers whose goodness and honesty help us become holy people. |
| All | We sing your praises, Lord. |
| Grade 4 | Thank you for these teachers who are filled with precious gifts. |
| All | We sing your praises, Lord. |
| Grade 5 | Thank you for these teachers whose knowledge makes everything new. |
| All | We sing your praises, Lord. |
| Grade 6 | Thank you for these teachers whose enthusiasm inspires us to become your prophets. |
| All | We sing your praises, Lord. |
| Grade 7 | Thank you for these teachers whose belief in us empowers us to be at home with Wisdom. |
| All | We sing your praises, Lord. |
| Grade 8 | Thank you for these teachers whose example shows us how to be Christ for one another. |
| All | We sing your praises, Lord. |
| Leader | Dear God, we sing your praises and celebrate your glory in the presence of these holy and gifted people. Let their example be a model for us all. Grant us the grace to go forth to learn well—the greatest gift we can give our teachers in return. We ask this in the perfect confidence and great hope given us by your Son, Jesus Christ, our Lord. |
| All | Amen. |

# Parent/ Teacher Meetings

This section is offered for those parent-teacher association meetings that are called at times of change in a school or religious education program. Those who facilitate these types of meetings may find these services helpful just as they are, but should feel free to adapt them for particular situations.

 # Guide Us in Your Service

**For times of discernment**

This prayer aims to offer more substance for discernment and action than a hastily voiced Our Father or Hail Mary.

**Call to Prayer**

| | |
|---|---|
| Leader | In the name of the Father, and of the Son, and of the Holy Spirit. |
| All | Amen. |
| Leader | Invisible but ever-present Lord, let us remember why we gather here, to work together to make this school a vibrant and living witness of all that we profess to believe. Help us discern wisely, listen thoughtfully, and take action prudently but courageously for the sake of our children, our church, and our world. |

**Reading    1 Peter 2:4–5, 9,17; 4:8–11**

| | |
|---|---|
| Reader 1 | Come to him a living stone, though rejected by mortals yet chosen and precious in God's sight, and like living stones, let yourselves be built into a spiritual house, to be a holy priesthood, to offer spiritual sacrifices acceptable to God through Jesus Christ. |
| Reader 2 | You are a chosen race, a royal priesthood, a holy nation, God's own people, in order that you may proclaim the mighty acts of him who called you out of darkness into his marvelous light. |
| Reader 3 | Honor everyone. Above all, maintain constant love for one another, for love covers a multitude of sins. Be hospitable to one another without complaining. Like good stewards of the manifold grace of God, serve one another with whatever gift each of you has received. |
| Reader 4 | Whoever speaks must do so as one speaking the very words of God; whoever serves must do so with the strength that God supplies, so that God may be glorified in all things through Jesus Christ. |
| Readers 1-4 | To him belong the glory and the power forever and ever. Amen. |
| | |
| Leader | As we gather to do your will, Lord, help us put aside any differences that may exist between us. May we look always toward the greater good. Hear us as we pray:  Guide us in your service, Lord. |
| All | Guide us in your service, Lord. |

## Intercessions

| | |
|---|---|
| Reader | When enthusiasm threatens to overcome good sense and reason |
| All | Guide us in your service, Lord. |
| Reader | When boredom threatens to hide our purpose from us |
| All | Guide us in your service, Lord. |
| Reader | When anger threatens to destroy our good hearts and good work |
| All | Guide us in your service, Lord. |
| Reader | When differing opinions threaten to make seeing eyes grow blind |
| All | Guide us in your service, Lord. |
| Reader | When calls from all sides threaten to deafen our ears to your voice |
| All | Guide us in your service, Lord. |
| Reader | When fatigue threatens to distract us from your call and your work |
| All | Guide us in your service, Lord. |
| Reader | When joy and high spirits break through our barriers and join all our territories as one |
| All | Guide us in your service, Lord. |
| | |
| Leader | Bless us, Lord, and hold us in your heart. Give us courage and strength to devote our lives and our work to you. Send your Spirit to us to uphold us in our service. Give us eyes to see and ears to hear, and discernment to bring about justice and peace in this place and in every place. |
| All | Amen. |

# Be with Us, Lord

## For healing

There are times when discord can break the best of associations apart into factions and camps. This prayer service was designed to remind everyone of their first responsibility and call—to work together for the good of the school and parish community.

## Call to Prayer

| | |
|---|---|
| Leader | In the name of the Father, and of the Son, and of the Holy Spirit. |
| All | Amen. |
| Leader | We gather together to sing God's praises, and to take part in the ministry of working to help make God's message come alive here in this place. May we grow ever more united in purpose, strength, and witness. The apostle Paul reminds us of our calling. |

## Reading    Colossians 3:12–17

| | |
|---|---|
| Reader 1 | As God's chosen ones, holy and beloved, clothe yourselves with compassion, kindness, humility, meekness, and patience. |
| Reader 2 | Bear with one another and, if anyone has a complaint against another, forgive each other; just as the Lord has forgiven you, so must you forgive. |
| Reader 3 | Above all, clothe yourselves with love, which binds everything together in perfect harmony. |
| Reader 4 | And let the peace of Christ rule in your hearts, to which indeed you were called in the one body. |
| Reader 1 | And be thankful. |
| Reader 2 | Let the word of Christ dwell in you richly; |
| Reader 3 | teach and admonish one another in all wisdom; |
| Reader 4 | and with gratitude in your hearts sing psalms, hymns, and spiritual songs to God. |
| Readers 1-4 | And whatever you do, in word or deed, do everything in the name of the Lord Jesus, giving thanks to God the Father through him. |
| | |
| Leader | Let our work together be a sign of the good news of Jesus to all we meet. We are confident that God will give us strength and guidance. In this sure and certain hope, let us respond: Be with us, Lord. |
| All | Be with us, Lord. |

## Intercessions

| | |
|---|---|
| Reader | Grant us the humility to be meek, the patience to be kind, and the will to be merciful. |
| All | Be with us, Lord. |
| Reader | Give us the mercy to forgive others as you forgive us, and to work always with hearts willing and eager to be united in purpose. |
| All | Be with us, Lord. |
| Reader | Grant us peace in our hearts so that your ever-present and all-encompassing love may reach out to others through our actions. |
| All | Be with us, Lord. |
| Reader | Help us work as one body, ever mindful of your glory. |
| All | Be with us, Lord. |
| Reader | Help us be ever thankful for all the blessings that surround us. Help us recognize them even when they seem hidden from our sight. |
| All | Be with us, Lord. |
| Reader | Let your word dwell in us, inspiring us and informing every action we undertake on your behalf. |
| All | Be with us, Lord. |
| Reader | Grant us wisdom to instruct in love and kindness. Keep our eyes focused on the work of your kingdom that our small tasks represent. |
| All | Be with us, Lord. |
| Reader | Let us always sing gratefully to you from our hearts, raising our voices in praise and thanksgiving, no matter how hard our task. |
| All | Be with us, Lord. |
| | |
| Leader | As we come together to praise your name and give you thanks, O Lord, let us always remember that we do this, and everything in our lives, in the name of Jesus, your Son. |
| All | Amen. |
| Leader | Let us take a moment to share with each other a sign of Christ's peace. (pause) With that peace dwelling in us, let us turn our hearts and minds to the work before us. |

# Make Us Worthy, Lord

**For inspiring people to service**

This prayer service was designed for times of organizational unity—e.g., gearing up for a school bazaar or festival, or any fundraising activity—to remind everyone of how this event might make a difference throughout the community, and be a testimony to God working in this place.

**Call to Prayer**

Leader In the name of the Father, and of the Son, and of the Holy Spirit.

All Amen.

Leader We gather here to do God's work, to enrich our community, and to make our school and parish a beacon for all who seek God's light and warmth. Let us pause for a moment to place ourselves in God's presence, and then listen to God's word.

**Reading** **Ephesians 2:19–22**

Reader 1 So then you are no longer strangers and aliens, but you are citizens with the saints and also members of the household of God.

Reader 2 You are built upon the foundation of the apostles and prophets, with Christ Jesus himself as the cornerstone.

Reader 3 In him the whole structure is joined together and grows into a holy temple in the Lord.

Reader 4 In the Lord, you also are built together spiritually into a dwelling-place for God.

Leader Dear Lord, you have chosen us to carry your word to others in all that we do. Let our work here together justify your confidence in us, your children, to make your love and mercy a reality for all in our community. Our work carries on a tradition built up over twenty centuries. We pray to be worthy of this calling. Let us raise our hopes and fears to God as we respond: Make us worthy, Lord.

All Make us worthy, Lord.

## Intercessions

| | |
|---|---|
| Reader | Let us rejoice in the wonder of our fellowship with all God's people. |
| All | Make us worthy, Lord. |
| Reader | Let us marvel at being members of God's family. |
| All | Make us worthy, Lord. |
| Reader | Let us wonder at being chosen to be part of the great city of God, and at the powerful witnesses who have gone before us. |
| All | Make us worthy, Lord. |
| Reader | Let us praise our cornerstone, Jesus Christ, through whom we are empowered to carry God's word to all. |
| All | Make us worthy, Lord. |
| Reader | Let us pray for unity, not division, to be a solid edifice that reflects your glory in our city, our diocese, and the universal Church. |
| All | Make us worthy, Lord. |
| Reader | Let us join together in harmony and fellowship, that we may be open to the Spirit's guidance and that the Spirit may find in us a happy place to reside. |
| All | Make us worthy, Lord. |
| Reader | Let us work always for justice, for holiness, for peace. Let our witness be honest and based on our solidarity with all our brothers and sisters. |
| All | Make us worthy, Lord. |
| Reader | Let us speak always in truth, seek always for the greater good, and proclaim always God's goodness through all our words and deeds, here and in our daily lives. |
| All | Make us worthy, Lord. |
| Reader | Let us live in love, so that all will recognize our parish as a place where God lives. |
| All | Make us worthy, Lord. |
| | |
| Leader | God, you make us the tools to bring the word of life to all. Make us worthy of this calling, through Jesus Christ, your Son. |
| All | Amen. |
| Leader | Let us take a moment to share a sign of peace with one another, and go forth to do God's work. |

# For Everything There Is a Season

**For a change of leadership**

In every parish and school's life comes a time when there is a change of leadership. These can be troubling and tense times. This prayer service is offered to help remind those in school and parish work of the importance of solidarity at these times, and of the need to remain united in support of the newcomer—which should make the transition much easier for all involved!

**Call to Prayer**

| | |
|---|---|
| Leader | In the name of the Father, and of the Son, and of the Holy Spirit. |
| All | Amen. |
| Leader | We come together to begin a new season in our school and parish life. We come united in trust of one another and united in the cause of helping to build God's kingdom here in this place. Let us take hope and vision from the words of James. |

**Reading**  **James 1:17–18, 21b–22, 27**

| | |
|---|---|
| Reader 1 | Every generous act of giving, with every perfect gift, is from above, coming down from the Father of lights, with whom there is no variation or shadow due to change. |
| Reader 2 | In fulfillment of his own purpose he gave us birth by the word of truth, so that we would become a kind of first fruits of his creatures. |
| Reader 3 | Welcome with meekness the implanted word that has the power to save your souls. |
| Reader 4 | But be doers of the word and not merely hearers who deceive themselves. Religion that is pure and undefiled before God, the Father, is this: |
| Readers 1-4 | to care for orphans and widows in their distress, and to keep oneself unstained by the world. |
| Leader | Lord, we seek your guidance and wisdom as we gather to do your will, and we pray, Make us doers of your word. |
| All | Make us doers of your word. |

## Intercessions

| | |
|---|---|
| Reader | Lord, we have many different gifts. Help us unite them in one common cause. |
| All | Make us doers of your word. |
| Reader | Lord, we put ourselves humbly in your presence. Make us worthy servants in your cause. |
| All | Make us doers of your word. |
| Reader | Lord, we come together as witnesses of your goodness. Let us share that goodness with all we meet. |
| All | Make us doers of your word. |
| Reader | Lord, let us be attentive to the needs of our own school and parish community. Help us find those who would not seek us out. |
| All | Make us doers of your word. |
| Reader | Lord, let our care for our own not blind us to the needs and worries of others. |
| All | Make us doers of your word. |
| Reader | Lord, let our voices be raised in the cause of justice for all our neighbors, wherever in the world they live. |
| All | Make us doers of your word. |
| Reader | Lord, help us always to remember our primary purpose in serving you, wherever and to whomever we are needed. |
| All | Make us doers of your word. |
| Reader | Lord, give us courage and strength to stand firm in our faith, against the prevailing concerns of society. Let us remember the poor, the orphaned, the widows. |
| All | Make us doers of your word. |
| Reader | Lord, grant us the light of your love, that we may share it with all we meet, and in all we do. |
| All | Make us doers of your word. |
| | |
| Leader | Lord of all generosity, hope, and love, we are here because your goodness to us inspires us to share that bounty with others. Help us to unite as a parish family, so that our only and constant aim will be to give you praise, honor, and glory, as we work together to make your kingdom come. |
| All | Amen. |
| Leader | As a sign of our commitment and purpose, let us exchange with one another a sign of Christ's peace. |

# Of Related Interest

## Weekday Liturgies for Children

*Creative Ways to Celebrate YearRound*
Mary Kathleen Glavich, SND

Offers an extensive array of guidelines, suggestions, and plans to promote child involvement in, and enjoyment of, the liturgy celebration.
0-89622-694-8, 248 pp, $39.95 (M-74)

## Celebrating Catholic Rites and Rituals in Religion Class

Kathy Chateau and Paula Miller

Focuses on the liturgical experiences of children within the Catholic tradition and includes suggestions for uses, prayer rituals and directions for teachers.
0-89622-939-4, 80 pp, $12.95 (J-10)

## Celebrating Seasons

*Prayer Lessons for Advent, Christmas, Lent and Easter*
Phyllis Vos Wezeman
and Jude Dennis Fournier

This easy-to-use format for prayer lessons explores themes such as seasonal traditions, cultural diversity, and missions.
1-58595-016-5, 80 pp, $12.95 (J-64)

## Praying with the Saints

*30 Classroom Prayer Service for Children*
Gwen Costello

These prayer services and activities focus on an aspect of a saint's life that children (grades 3-6) can imitate.
0-89622-982-3, 104 pp, $12.95 (J-30)

**Available at religious bookstores or from:**

# TWENTY-THIRD PUBLICATIONS

**A Division of Bayard**  PO BOX 180 · MYSTIC, CT 06355
1-800-321-0411 · FAX: 1-800-572-0788 · E-MAIL: ttpubs@aol.com
www.twentythirdpublications.com

**Call for a free catalog**